Block

Cryptocurrency

By United Library

https://campsite.bio/unitedlibrary

Table of Contents

Disclaimer

This biography book is a work of nonfiction based on the public life of a famous person. The author has used publicly available information to create this work. While the author has thoroughly researched the subject and attempted to depict it accurately, it is not meant to be an exhaustive study of the subject. The views expressed in this book are those of the author alone and do not necessarily reflect those of any organization associated with the subject. This book should not be taken as an endorsement, legal advice, or any other form of professional advice. This book was written for entertainment purposes only.

Introduction

Discover the transformative power of blockchain and cryptocurrency in this essential guide to the technology redefining the financial landscape. Immerse yourself in the complex world of blockchain, a revolutionary distributed ledger system that offers unrivalled security and transparency by chaining records through cryptographic hashes. Understand the genesis of blockchain technology, initiated by the enigmatic Satoshi Nakamoto for Bitcoin, and explore its evolution from a digital currency facilitator to a foundation for a myriad of applications beyond cryptocurrencies.

Navigate the complexities of cryptocurrency, a revolutionary digital asset designed to function as a medium of exchange without reliance on central authorities such as governments or banks. Learn about the complex mechanisms that secure and verify transactions through advanced cryptography, ensuring that every currency property is accurately recorded in a decentralized ledger. From the creation of Bitcoin to the explosion of over 25,000 cryptocurrencies by 2023, grasp the potential and challenges associated with this digital financial frontier.

Whether you're a curious novice to the subject of digital currencies or a seasoned investor looking to deepen your knowledge of blockchain technology, this guide offers a comprehensive overview of the basic concepts, technologies and implications of blockchain and cryptocurrency. Discover why these innovations are more than just technical marvels, but are redefining the way we think about money, privacy and trust in the digital age.

Don't miss your chance to become an expert in the digital revolution that is blockchain and cryptocurrency. Discover the potential to transform your understanding of money and technology.

Get your guide to blockchain and cryptocurrency today, and join the digital finance revolution!

Blockchain

A **blockchain** is a technology for storing and transmitting information without a central authority. Technically, it is a distributed database in which the information sent by users and the links within the database are verified and grouped into blocks at regular intervals, thus forming a chain. The whole system is secured by cryptography. By extension, a blockchain is a distributed database that manages a list of records protected against falsification or modification by the storage nodes; it is therefore a distributed and secure record of all transactions carried out since the start-up of the distributed system.

There is an analogy with the Internet, as in both cases the technologies employ computer protocols linked to a decentralized infrastructure. While the Internet enables data packets to be transferred from a "secure" server to remote clients (with the recipients responsible for verifying the integrity of the transmitted data), a blockchain enables "trust" to be established between separate agents of the system. With blockchain technology, the "trusted third party" becomes the system itself: each distributed element of the blockchain contains the elements needed to guarantee the integrity of the data exchanged (via a cryptographic algorithm).

Concepts and definitions

A blockchain is fundamentally a shared database, which is why it is represented by the concept of a distributed ledger (although distributed ledgers can be based on other technologies). Blockchain differs from traditional database technology: instead of a single database managed by a single owner who shares the data, in the blockchain network network participants have their own copy of the database. A secure consensus algorithm can ensure unanimous agreement on the correct content of the data, ensure the conformity of the agreed copies of the data, and ensure the subsequent absence of cheating through data alteration.

This enables a number of people or entities - collaborators or competitors - to agree on a consensus of information, and to immutably record this consensus of truth. For this reason, blockchain has been described as a "trust infrastructure".

ISO standardization

The term is so widely used that it is sometimes stripped of its substance.

To avoid this, standards have been defined.

- ISO 22739:2020: *Blockchain and* distributed ledger technologies - Vocabulary

- ISO/TR 23244:2020 : *Blockchain and distributed ledger technologies - Privacy and personally identifiable information protection considerations*

- ISO/TR 23455:2019 : *Blockchain and distributed ledger technologies - Overview of and interactions between smart contracts in blockchain and distributed ledger technology systems*

- ISO/TR 23576:2020 : *Blockchain and distributed ledger technologies - Security management of digital asset custodians*

The ISO standard also defines 84 vocabulary terms.

History

Previous work

The first study of cryptographically secure blockchains was described in 1991 by Haber (en) and Stornetta (en). They wanted to implement a system where time-stamped documents could not be falsified or backdated. In 1992, Bayer (en), Haber and Stornetta incorporated the Merkle tree concept into the system, which improved its efficiency by allowing multiple documents to be assembled into a single block.

According to researcher Ittai Abraham, the first decentralized certification system is that of Surety, which has been publishing a cryptographic certificate from its database in the "Classifieds and Lost & Found" section of *The New York Times* every week since 1995.

The first blockchain applied to a crypto-currency was conceptualized by a person (or team) known as Satoshi Nakamoto in 2008. It was implemented the following year by Nakamoto as the main component of bitcoin, where it serves as the public ledger for all transactions on the network.

Emergence

Since then, many virtual currencies and cryptocurrencies have been using blockchains for their security. Transactions on a blockchain are virtually impossible to reverse, because blockchains are resistant to change.

After 2008, blockchain and the crypto-currencies that depend on it - with no legal tender central bank and no defined territory of exchangeability - were often presented as an almost miraculous source of enrichment, arousing the interest of the stock market then plunged into the doldrums of the 2008 crisis. Many companies then rebranded themselves by incorporating the word "blockchain" or "bitcoin" into their new name (a procedure that is illegal in some countries, including the USA, as it could amount to misinformation and false advertising). A study, published in Economics Letters in August 2019, showed that these companies gain significantly in notoriety or value for two months, but that this effect fades and then reverses to a negative effect (within five months of the change). The authors urge investors to be cautious about companies changing their name before actually investing in blockchain, as these cosmetic name changes are generally only intended to capitalize on "the hysteria surrounding the rise in bitcoin prices".

In the USA, numerous companies have been summoned before the Securities and Exchange Commission (SEC) for including the term "blockchain" in their name in the absence of a clear link with the domain. Bioptix, for example, became Riot Blockchain, which moved from the veterinary field to Bitcoin's banking service (cryptocurrency mining).

In 2023, blockchain-recorded transactions are used by banks to carry out central bank fund transfers.

Aspects

Reliability

Like the crypto-currencies it forms the backbone of, blockchain is almost always presented in the media as immutable, impossible to hack and fraud-proof.

While in the 2020s some suggest replacing all or part of financial audits (or other types of audits) with blockchains, one study (2020) wanted to check whether in fact the degree of security of crypto-currencies and blockchain registries is as high as is generally claimed.

The authors, Castonguay and Stein Smith, compiled and studied existing literature on initial cryptocurrency offerings, security levels, theft and hacking of blockchains and blockchain-based platforms or in crypto-currency wallets. They concluded, "Contrary to the popular press, we find that in practice, blockchain and crypto-currencies are more prone to malfeasance, fraud and manipulation than is generally thought. The security and trust provided by blockchain as a technological tool is no more secure than the underlying code that establishes the blockchain, and the value derived from crypto-currencies is no more reliable than the entity developing the crypto-currency. Neither is without vulnerabilities. Skepticism and appropriate due diligence must be maintained for any entity seeking to use blockchain technology or invest in crypto-currencies."

In other words, the reliability of blockchain depends largely on the method used to secure it, and is not automatically immutable.

According to financial professionals, the quality of data audited and stored "in chain" is considerably lower than that of financial statements resulting from a real audit.

In June 2022, a report funded by the U.S. Defense Advanced Research Projects Agency (DARPA) indicated that a blockchain may be dependent on a single online banking player (an overly centralized blockchain) that exploits weaknesses in security properties (low implementation quality at other banking players).

Social impact of blockchains

Blockchain is often presented as a trust-generating, mathematical and computational miracle solution which, when placed at the service of various socio-technical systems, has strong potential for socially useful transformation, such as traceability in supply chains, e-procurement and arts trading or health data management; "smart contract" (whose social impacts are still debated); sustainability tools (which in 2019 had not yet been able to prove itself, for lack of reliable and accessible data). However, its uses (for financial assets in particular) are not yet regulated, and its rapidly increasing energy consumption, as well as its contribution to global CO_2 emissions via several types of use, raise questions about its socio-environmental sustainability.

Blockchain presents itself as "technologically neutral", but according to cyber philosopher Michel Bauwens in Le Monde (2016), "technology is never neutral. It is a terrain of conflict influenced by the imaginations and interests of those responsible for its design. Blockchain thus derives from a very particular vision of man: autonomous individuals enter into contracts with each other. They don't need a collective, a community. And contracts are based on a form of ownership. As in Monopoly, you can't play without chips. An Indian peasant in Uttar Pradesh, who doesn't have a computer, is excluded. The ideology takes on an anarcho-capitalist connotation, coupled with an American-style libertarian vision". What's more, to supposedly create trust between two people, blockchain requires verification of the entire network. "It's crazy! Because of the energy expended, but also in terms of human trust", trust which, on the contrary, is the basis of peer-to-peer as used in the collaborative economy and the commons, open source, crowdsourcing, Fablabs, micro-factories, the *makers* movement, urban agriculture, etc., which, according to Bauwens, would open the way to a post-capitalist society.

Blockchain wanted to dispense with intermediaries, but it shifts trust from traditional intermediaries (bankers, notaries, energy service companies, etc.) to the technology, the code (which may contain bugs) and therefore to those who develop it (miners and software developers in particular) and electricity suppliers... "with what social risks?" ask Energy-Cities and Ademe in 2018; with what possible biases of overconfidence towards digital technology? "Will we prefer these new intermediaries - which could also be a major gateway for the GAFAs (Google, Amazon, Facebook, Apple)?

According to its promoters, blockchain could facilitate the fight against tax fraud (for example, according to two researchers in Dubai, via a personal and corporate tax system setting a predetermined rate linked to gross income rather than net income), collect and manage taxes (which was proposed in China in 2020 by Juan Wang, of Jilin University - without success -, etc.), or help banks, states and companies verify the compliance, probity and integrity of individuals/clients with regard to legislation aimed at preventing corruption, identity theft, various frauds, money laundering, etc.), or help banks, states and companies to verify the compliance, probity and integrity of individuals/customers with regard to legislation aimed at preventing corruption, identity theft, various forms of fraud, money laundering, fake news or even the financing of terrorism.

In fact, crypto-currencies have been rapidly used for illegitimate activities such as money laundering, financial scams, war and terrorism financing and tax evasion. The scale of tax evasion in Europe is unknown, as is the extent to which virtual currencies are misused for this purpose. Prior to 2010, tax evasion is estimated to have exceeded 7 billion euros.

In 2022, when "more than 100 million people hold crypto-currencies, mainly as speculative assets", Howson and de Vries state: "the unsustainable trajectory of some crypto-currencies is having a disproportionate impact on poor and vulnerable communities where crypto-currency producers and other actors take advantage of economic instabilities, weak regulations and access to cheap energy and other resources [...] If the mass adoption of bitcoin continues, an escalation of the climate crisis is inevitable, disproportionately exacerbating social and environmental challenges for communities already experiencing multiple dimensions of deprivation." Some states or regions are experiencing a "mining rush"; the high volatility of crypto-currencies and the vagaries of mining can plunge the least well-trained and/or hardware-equipped miners into bankruptcy, even though they have sometimes left their trade in the hope of enriching themselves in the process (thus, in 2018, the total market capitalization of all crypto-currencies reached $728 billion, but just three weeks after this peak, it plummeted to around $360 billion). Energy-intensive mining often benefits from advantageous tariffs (for example, the Canadian group Hut 8 claims to have 100,000 machines in operation in three mining centers by 2022 (i.e. 127.5 peta hashes per second) and secure electricity at a very low price (3.5 cents per kWh on average) for 209 MW of contracted electricity purchase capacity.

Blockchain can have positive effects or lead to serious abuses (particularly if used against democracy, for example for the social credit system or other forms of surveillance and control of citizens in authoritarian or dictatorial regimes).

Blockchain, sustainable city and smartcity

Blockchain is often brought to the fore in smartcities, particularly for managing energy flows and bills, and in particular intermittent renewable energies (solar, wind, with blockchains being tested in participatory projects, including one based on Ethereum, see dedicated cryptocurrencies such as *SolarCoin, Gruenstromjeton, NRGCoin*). In 2017, Wien Energie, Vienna's energy utility, was testing a blockchain to manage energy trading in the market; but according to Andrew Collinge (head of *Smart Cities* at the Greater London Authority), city leaders need to "better prepare for the implications of technologies such as blockchain; while they may have a high-level understanding of the technology, there is generally 'no understanding' of the impact it could have for government and the communities it serves. This absolutely has to change [...] There is an urgent need for utilities, and the leadership of those utilities, to be able to anticipate the technology and the disrupted business models it creates; and that it can respond by setting out the key claims."

Carbon footprint of blockchains, effects on the climate

The British Blockchain Association argued in 2018 that blockchain could help enforce certain climate targets, but mining is denounced by others as a climate catastrophe; for example, according to a study published in 2017 in the scientific journal *Nature Climate Change*, Bitcoin use emitted over 69 million tonnes of carbon dioxide (CO_2) in 2017, equivalent to Ireland's CO_2 output or around 0.3% of global greenhouse gas production.

In 2018 MIT of Cambridge University, Stoll, Klaaßen and Gallersdörfer of the Center for Energy and Environmental Policy Research estimated the energy footprint of Bitcoin mining: in November 2018, it alone would have required 48.2 TWh of electrical power, equivalent to 21.5 to 53.6 MtCO2 emitted in the year (a level that has since worsened, but was then comparable to those of Bolivia or Portugal). That same year (2018), Cédric Villani notes in his report that "almost 4% of global carbon emissions are due to the production and use of digital tools, which generate energy consumption increasing by 8.5% per year, and its share of global electricity consumption (growing by 2% per year) could reach 20% (moderate scenario) or 50% (pessimistic scenario) in 2030, and thus be multiplied by ten in twenty years. Given the global electricity mix, the share of greenhouse gas (GHG) emissions generated by the digital sector is set to rise from 2.5% in 2015 to 5% in 2020 (2.5 Gt).

In 2021, according to Digiconomist (estimate of 64.18 MtCO2 emitted by Bitcoin, published in July 2021, i.e. approximately the carbon footprint of Greece or the Sultanate of Oman) and according to *Cambridge* University's CBECI (*Cambridge Bitcoin Energy Consumption*) index, the carbon and environmental footprint of several blockchains is growing at a worrying rate (those, cumulatively, of Bitcoin and Ethereum were estimated in July 2021 at 90.31 MtCO2 ; almost as much as Belgium's cumulative emissions: 91.20 MtCO2).

By 2022, Bitcoin mining has "a carbon footprint that has single-handedly surpassed that of the gold mining industry", while in terms of value creation, Bitcoin is less attractive than mining copper, gold, platinum and even rare earth oxides. In 2018, Krause compared the energy required to produce one US dollar (US$) of digital assets between January 1, 2016 and June 30, 2018 to that required to produce the same value from real metal deposits. Mining Bitcoin, Ethereum, Litecoin and Monero respectively consumed (on average) 17, 7, 7 and 14 MJ to generate US$1, more than conventional mining of copper, gold, platinum and rare earth oxides, 122, 4, 5, 7 and 9 megajoules (MJ) respectively. Cryptocurrencies already consume significantly more energy than mining these minerals, and although the cryptocurrency market is rather volatile, network hash rates for three of the four cryptocurrencies have been steadily increasing, suggesting that their energy requirements will increase further (necessarily for Bitcoin). According to this assessment, in thirty months, the mining of these four cryptocurrencies would have caused the emission of between 3 and 15 million tonnes of CO_2 , a considerable amount of greenhouse gases.

Energy and environmental aspects

In the wake of the banking and financial crisis of autumn 2008, Bitcoin set out to be an irreversible, unforgeable, decentralized, anonymized and participative electronic payment system, based on a self-managed mutualist infrastructure, insensitive to borders and digital attacks, and resilient (because it is decentralized and redundant). The aim was to be independent of banks, central banks, states, pressure groups or other third parties.

But by securing his blockchain with "proof of work", Satoshi Nakamoto (supposed inventor of Bitcoin) has subjected himself to an external resource that he cannot control: electricity; a resource unevenly distributed around the world and subject to hazards, which has a limited cost and availability, and which mining essentially transforms into heat, which can however be reused.

According to Bob Burnett (in, *Bitcoin Magazine,* February 21, 2022), this is Bitcoin's main "Achilles heel": it now has too much need for hash power density in too few mining farms (which are also increasingly expensive). For example, Atlas Power intends to build a mining capacity of around 750 megawatts (MW) on servers with a capacity of at least 150 tera per second (TH/s) in Williston, a cold, arid area of North Dakota, also known for its oil shale, before the end of 2023, at a cost of $1.9 billion. In 2014, the town had to acquire 112 MW of additional (fossil-fired) power generation, and the miners there are demanding an additional 750 megawatts. This type of "recentralization" combined with hyper-consumption of electricity massively exposes Bitcoin to the risk of an attack on the entire system, simply by denying electricity supply. And other recentralization factors are added to this one (geopolitics, jurisdictions, type of energy sources, size of mining farms, nature and ownership of "mining pools", or even the origin of microchips, added B. Burnett in February 2021).

In fact, a blockchain's electricity demand varies by several orders of magnitude depending on its architecture, size, type of mining hardware and the value taken by a cryptocurrency. In the case of Bitcoin, Satochi has chosen the most energy-intensive form of security, which can only become more and more energy-intensive as Bitcoin increases in value. This has led to the creation of many costly mining farms (in the millions to over a billion dollars per site for the largest), costly in terms of chips and hardware, and which have paradoxically become highly vulnerable to the risks of attacks, administrative closures or, more simply, power cuts by the supplier. The disappearance of a mining farm would not pose a problem, but, notes Bob Burnett, a coordinated attack (a simple power cut) against the most important farms would deprive bitcoin of the energy resources that are vital to maintain the chain's processing time per block (a time that Satochi has set at around 10 minutes). This crisis scenario is all the more credible given that miners' pools have concentrated their farms in a few welcoming countries, but many of which have authoritarian governance and/or are politically unstable (e.g. Kazakhstan, Russia, Georgia) or have a weak currency (the Venezuelan bolivar lost 99.9% of its value between 2016 and 2018, and the state limits the country's supply of hard currency, which has encouraged Bitcoin mining by Venezuelans who see it as a safer investment than their national currency). In the USA, elected officials and communities in Texas and North Dakota, Kentucky, Illinois and Georgia have recently (2021, 2022) shown themselves to be very welcoming to mining farms, but these will be dependent on fossil resources (electricity largely derived from oil or gas and therefore highly carbon-intensive), and a fragile power grid (systemic blackout) and vulnerable to directed terrorist attacks and/or increasingly frequent natural disasters, which could jeopardize the mining network there. Although the climate is not conducive to mining, and electricity is highly carbon-intensive, Rockland (Texas), thanks to cheap electricity, has managed to attract America's largest bitcoin mining farm (operated by Whinstone US, since acquired by Riot Blockchain). Georgia, following a tripartite agreement between mining companies ISW Holdings, Bit5ive, and Bitmain, hopes to attract 56,000 Bitmain miners by October 2022, but is competing with other states that offer miners tax breaks, going so far as to offer zero-rated electricity to attract them.

The red bar chart (opposite) provides a rough comparison of the power consumption of different types of blockchain architectures. It shows that there is a huge difference (of several orders of magnitude) between the low power consumption generated by an average transaction processed by a "normal" server, and that generated by blockchain systems, particularly when the chain is based on "proof of work", as is typically the case with Bitcoin, which is by far the most energy-intensive cryptocurrency.

And its operating principle intrinsically condemns it to become even more so as Bitcoin grows and/or increases in value).

Consumption by mining farms was so intense in Kazakhstan in 2021, that it competed with domestic, urban and industrial electricity needs causing power cuts (according to the government mining increased Kazakhstan's electricity consumption by 7% to 8% in one year; this justified stoppages in electricity delivery to cryptocurrency miners). The example of mainland China shows that mining can suddenly be banned in a country. In China before the ban, many "miners" moved their facilities seasonally: from late autumn to spring ("dry season") they were in the most stable coal-fired regions (typically Xinjiang), then in the "rainy season" they migrated to regions with temporary hydroelectric overcapacity (typically Sichuan) where electricity was supplied at low cost.

The consumption of a blockchain is very difficult to assess on a miner-by-miner basis, since blockchains are based on a large number of open, distributed networks, where we know neither the precise number of participants (which can fluctuate at any time), nor the characteristics of their computers and servers, nor the intensity of their mining effort, nor sometimes the energy sources used to generate the electricity, let alone the grey energy required for the entire process. What's more, miners working to solve the puzzles of a bitcoin-type blockchain will use dedicated chips ("*Application-specific integrated circuits*" or ASICS), specially adapted to the *SHA256* cryptographic hash chosen for Bitcoin, whereas - conversely - a digital currency like Ethereum has been designed to prevent the use of such highly dedicated circuits for specific mining.

Nevertheless, according to Vranken (2017) and Krause and Tolaymat (2018), the low and high limits of direct energy consumption of any PoW blockchain can be quite finely assessed, indirectly :

1. the lower limit of the energy requirement for mining alone for a PoW blockchain is linked to the difficulty of the cryptographic puzzles and the frequency with which they are solved, both of which are known parameters; we can therefore deduce the value of the minimum frequency of calculations ("hash-rate") required to solve these puzzles. As an example, on February 5, 2020, data extracted from CoinMarketCap (2020) and Coinswitch (2019) show that at least 6.8 GW were needed on that day, (which would correspond to an annual requirement of at least 60 TWh, down to 54.02 TWh by March 19, 2021; and this is only the low end of the estimate, the high end being 319.40 TWh). This method can be used to

calculate the requirement considered over other
time periods;

2. the upper limit of the energy requirements of the
    mining process for a PoW blockchain can also be
    approached: if miners are rational and do not
    work at a loss (i.e. the expected revenue from
    mining remains higher than the associated costs,
    notably linked to the price of electricity).

For O'Dwyer & Malone (2014), blockchain-based systems
with proof-of-work are "energy guzzlers". And the use of
proof-of-work induces a consumption of electricity and
computing time (and therefore a mobilization of servers
or networks of individual computers) that is growing
worldwide. The Bank for International Settlements (the
"bank of central banks") has criticized the system of proof-
of-work validations required for blockchain; a system
described as an "environmental disaster" by Hyun Song
Shin in June 2018.

In 2015, Nicholas Weaver (International Computer Science
Institute; University of California at Berkeley), after
examining the online security of blockchain and the
energy efficiency of the "proof-of-work" system used by
blockchains concludes in both cases, that these solutions
are "totally inadequate".

In 2017, energy and blockchain analysts are worried about the possibility of a "*perfect* storm", because while energy efficiency gains in mining equipment are slowing down, the value of bitcoin and bitcoin transactions are rising (which dramatically increases the need for mining and therefore electricity. Already, some mining farms consume as much electricity as a small town. This problem worries, for example, Michael Reed (head of blockchain technology at Intel) and Peter Fairley (La Sapienza University), who compares Bitcoin to a leech "sucking" the contents of the world's power grids, and which will not be able to be contained for long by the rapid energy efficiency gains of mining. This was confirmed two years later by another (German) model of various possible scenarios; Beck et al. emphasized the need for detailed data on the energy consumption of blockchain technologies.

In 2018, several studies highlighted the risks posed by the fact that Bitcoin, and the way it operates, is intrinsically and intentionally designed to be a high consumer of electricity, making it a high emitter of calories and a contributor to global greenhouse gas emissions, at a time when international commitments are to decarbonize. It also competes with other uses of electricity. All this means that "Bitcoin's great transactional, trust and security benefits are overshadowed by the intentionally resource-hungry design of its transaction verification process, which now threatens the climate we depend on for our survival (...) at a time when the world's governments are scrambling to reduce energy consumption through their Paris Agreement climate change commitments and beyond to mitigate the consequences of climate change for the future."

In 2018, the computing power required to solve a Bitcoin puzzle more than tripled, resulting in a sharp rise in electricity consumption. In *Pour la Science*, Jean-Paul Delahaye talks about "Bitcoin's electrical madness". In Nature Climate Change, Mora et al (2018) show that if the trend continues at the rate of adoption of other widely adopted technologies, then "- on its own - Bitcoin will produce enough CO_2 emissions to push warming above 2°C in less than three decades". This model is challenged in 2019 by Dittmar and A. Praktiknjo, who wondered whether these emissions could cause warming to exceed +2°C by 2100. According to Masanet & al. in September 2019, these projections were deemed implausible and would overestimate Bitcoin's CO_2 emissions, at least in the short term. Mora et al. respond to their critics in 2019.

According to Cédric Villani's 2018 report, generally speaking "by 2040, the energy required for computing needs is also expected to exceed global energy production. Advances in blockchain could also cause our energy needs to explode. It is therefore vital to raise awareness of these issues and take action to prevent shortages".

In 2019, Ethereum (with a power demand of 0.6 to 3 GW) tends to reach Bitcoin's level of power consumption, and according to Jade & al. (2019) in the event of linear growth in block difficulty and a sigmoidal increase in mining hardware efficiency will consume around 8 GW in 2025. In 2020, four researchers from the *Project Group Business and Information Systems Engineering (BISE)* at Fraunhofer FIT, Bayreuth, Germany and/or the FIM Research Center at the University of Bayreuth, published a review of studies on the subject. In it, they conclude that the energy currently consumed (i.e. in the decade 2010) by blockchain is "effectively an amount of energy that can be considered disproportionate to the actual utility of the currencies". According to the authors, new approaches can theoretically reduce blockchain emissions by several orders of magnitude (compared to first-generation *Proof of Work*, or "PoW", blockchains), thanks to "alternative consensus mechanisms" (the "consensus mechanism" is the mechanism that enables agreement to be reached on which new blocks to add) but stress the authors, "in addition to consensus, the redundancy underlying all types of blockchain technology can make blockchain-based computing solutions considerably more energy-intensive than a centralized alternative without blockchain". This is because blockchain relies on mining, which is rewarded with a crypto-currency sum and fees for associated transactions; this sum is proportional to the market price of the crypto-currency. This means that, on the one hand, the longer the blockchain grows and integrates new blocks, the more energy it consumes, and, on the other hand, the more a crypto-currency gains in value on the financial markets, the more mining (PoW) is encouraged - mining which is the key to the system's inviolability, but which is by nature highly energy-intensive. By means of a simple positive feedback loop, the more valuable a PoW crypto-currency becomes, the better protected it is against attacks, but the more energy it consumes, potentially exponentially. Sedlmeir *et al.* in 2020 emphasize this point: "The high energy consumption of PoW blockchains is neither the result of inefficient algorithms nor obsolete hardware. It is striking that these blockchains are 'energy-intensive by design'", in particular to reduce vulnerability to attack by the 51%.

Kazakhstan has become the world's second-largest Bitcoin miner (following the ban on cryptocurrency mining and trading in China, which by the end of 2020 was home to over 60% of global mining for Bitcoin alone), hosting 18% of global activity by 2021, just behind the USA (35%) and ahead of Russia (11%), according to Cambridge University, which has posted an online calculator estimating the electrical power demand of the Bitcoin network (data updated every 24 hours). According to a documentary, the 50,000 mining machines then installed in one of the country's largest mining centers (set up under eight sheds near the town of Ekibastouz in a humid continental climate where the average monthly temperature does not exceed 22°C in summer, and directly supplied with high-voltage electricity by the local coal-fired power plant) consumed the equivalent of a town of around 100,000 inhabitants.

In 2022, Bitcoin mining will require as much energy as the whole of Thailand, and according to the Ethereum FAQ: "For example, it is estimated that Bitcoin and Ethereum burn over a million dollars in electricity and hardware costs per day as part of their consensus mechanism". In all cases, however, *sharding* always implies a transaction verification load intensity proportional to the amount of capital invested, and therefore increasing energy consumption.

Legal aspects

Blockchain raises legal issues. These include competition law, privacy law, intellectual property law, contract law and blockchain governance.

In particular, blockchains with public governance operate without trusted third parties, corresponding to a form of community idealism. They differ from consortium blockchains, where the nodes participating in the consensus are defined in advance, as in the R3 project.

A private blockchain operates with an established framework whose rules, if any, extrinsic to the code, govern its operation, whereas a public blockchain defines no rules other than those of the code constituted by the protocol and software technology of which it is composed.

The emergence of these new concepts implies the establishment of new forms of property, such as digital property, which can provide new sources of revenue. However, the question arises of how to capture and protect the digital rights exchanged. Jurist and Doctor of Law Sabine Van Haecke Lepic suggests *"incorporating a Metavers clause and an informed consent clause into the smart contract as the answer to making these rights enforceable and interoperable across various Metavers."*

Various authors, including for example legal scholar and Internet activist Primavera De Filippi (of the CNRS and Harvard University's "Berkman Klein Center for Internet & Society") and Samer Hassan in 2018, are calling for regulation, moving from a "*code is law*" stage to a "*law is code*" stage. But the legal changes could be considerable. In the energy sector alone, a study by PwC, commissioned by the North Rhine-Westphalia consumer representation (Verbraucherzentrale NRW), concluded that creating a legal and political framework conducive to the massification of blockchain in this sector would require significant changes to current legislation.

In 2018, a CNIL report found that blockchain does not *a priori* pose a problem, except with regard to the right to erasure of personal data, imposed by the General Data Protection Regulation.

Violations of privacy and personal data protection

At the crossroads of archival theory, privacy, financial governance and the emerging law of Internet Governance and Digital Information Governance, blockchain poses new legal problems, in particular because :

- Barring a general failure of the Internet, every block of the blockchain, once validated by the *miners*, is unalterable for eternity (i.e. it cannot be corrected, which is contrary to the right to be forgotten). This assertion is theoretical; in reality it is difficult but possible as soon as the majority of miners agree to modify the chain, as was the case with TheDAO, for example, after an attacker stole millions of Ethers by taking advantage of a vulnerability in the smart contract code;

- a blockchain has no internal regulatory authority (its computer code is its only law), no ombudsman, and it often seems to escape national laws, although China has banned it.

- in a *Bitcoin-type* system, players are generally identified by pseudonyms and always by anonymous addresses (a sequence of letters and numbers), and the information linked to a transaction recorded in the decentralized register provides little or no information on the general context of the exchange. While the information (before or after validation of the block containing it) is not directly accessible to the general public, it is, in an unlimited manner, accessible to miners ("every peer on the network has his or her own copy of the blockchain"). The ease of access to the quantity of personal information and metadata stored in the blockchain's "ledger" is also highly "asymmetrical", as it requires the necessary software and skills to retrieve it.

- The blockchain can formally prove that a specific piece of data or information has been recorded at a given time, but it does not indicate the substantive veracity or honesty of the transaction thus stored. It has been proposed that all diplomas, copyrights and patents should be recorded in blockchains, but a diploma acquired through undetected cheating, or a stolen or plagiarized work, or a dishonest patent, will be recorded in the same way as an honestly acquired diploma, or an original work, or a justified patent. In the same way, a judicial error could be registered quasi-definitively in a blockchain recording judicial acts. Land or notary registration in a developing country that does not yet have an accurate cadastre would have the same limitations: according to a study published in 2016, a digital cadastre on blockchain - even benefiting from an appropriate security architecture and infrastructure management controls - "does not guarantee the reliability of the information in the first place, and would have several limitations as a long-term solution for maintaining reliable digital records".

As a ledger, blockchain must comply with the GDPR, but its intrinsic characteristics also bring it into direct conflict with privacy and data protection, and in particular with :

- certain requirements of the General Data Protection Regulation (GDPR) (which imposes an obligation of result and not of means, remaining "technology-neutral"). Blockchain is not a search engine, so it is not legally subject to the right to be forgotten, but its access interfaces (as soon as they link an identity to a transaction) could be. However, the design of a blockchain makes it intrinsically impossible to delete any false, illicit or inappropriate content stored in one of the chain's blocks, except through coordinated action by the majority of individual nodes, which seems difficult in the case of large chains and when there is - in principle - no central actor. As Jude C. Umeh observed in 2016, no one is held responsible for the non-application of the right to be forgotten on the blockchain, unless all miners and/or software designers are held responsible;

- "the right to dereference also known as the *right to forget*" (a right enshrined in European law that allows the correction of inaccurate, inadequate or excessive information, to enable forgiveness and rehabilitation); socio-environmental impacts and the carbon footprint of major crypto-currencies, etc.), subjects of interest to many investors concerned about the ethical implications and environmental impacts of their investment choices. According to Primavera de Filippi and Michel Reymond, a blockchain like Steem.it's, which connects identities more directly to the information it "freezes", could be subject to the right to be forgotten.

Ways to slow the rise in mining-related consumption

Since the late 2010s, several avenues for reducing the intrinsic redundancy of blockchains have been explored in order to reduce their high energy consumption.

A first, forward-looking step is to better assess the growing and worrying impacts; environmental and climatic, but also in terms of waste and production of electronic waste generated by the Blockchain, while better understanding the factors that exacerbate these effects. Researchers have built predictive models to this end (for example, one such study, based on Facebook's Prophet algorithm and/or "deep neural networks" recently concluded that block size in blockchain is one of the main sources of energy waste and waste production).

A priori, reduction possibilities seem negligible for blockchains based on proof-of-work, as they intrinsically use redundancy (and therefore the cost and finite availability of energy) for their security: fraud must be so costly in terms of energy consumption that it deters any fraudster.

Mining hardware has already evolved from CPUs, to GPUs and then FPGAs and ASICs (dedicated chips) in the case of Bitcoin-type 'currencies'. Its level of performance and energy efficiency has risen sharply, but Dutch researcher Harald Vranken (in October 2017) nevertheless expects this trend to slow down. What's more, this progress is being negatively offset by the increasing computational and energy requirements of blockchains (rebound effect).

Ben-Sasson and colleagues, at a 2019 cryptocurrency conference, suggest creating other types of blockchains (or related network systems) based on zero-knowledge disclosure proof. In their view, they are promising because they are based on a much less energy-intensive consensus-seeking system, including for large networks: SNARKS, STARKS and other Zero-Knowledge proof systems require far less verification and communication overload on the chain, and therefore less electricity consumption, while maintaining a good level of security because every transaction is always verified by every node.

- Some datacenters use immersion cooling, which is claimed to reduce cooling energy consumption by 41% (according to US company LiquidStack, March 19, 2022), but the savings will only be temporary in the event of a rebound effect or exponential blockchain growth.

- In early 2021, four researchers from Germany and Luxembourg are proposing that mining (and/or other computationally-intensive activities, such as AWS computations to "educate" machine learning algorithms) use "surplus" electricity from intermittent renewable energy sources (as an alternative to electricity storage). Mining integrated into certain solar or wind farms (in cold regions) could thus improve energy flexibility and help stabilize the power grid. At the same time, it would reduce its carbon footprint, improve its environmental image and could even, as proposed by Utz et al. in 2019, help manage shared energy asset contracts via a Blockchain, or as proposed by two logistics economists Wu and Tran in 2018 help certify carbon emissions trading. This is interesting only if mining (of Bitcoin, for example) can remain profitable for the miner while his installation works intermittently to adjust to electricity (over)production and possibly the price of electricity. However, miners are only financially rewarded when they solve the calculations (puzzles) before their competitors.

- Another approach is to replace proof-of-work with proof-of-stake (PoS), i.e. a method based on another type of distributed consensus, more rational and less energy-consuming. Peercoin was the first proof-of-stake-based crypto-currency, then other methods were tried with BitShares, Gridocin, ShadowCash, Nxt, BlackCoin, NuShares/NuBits and Qora. Announced in 2015, then expected since 2018-2019, Ethereum made its transition to proof-of-stake ("The Merge" project) on September 15, 2022. Peercoin and Decred have opted for a hybrid PoW/PoS solution to maintain a robust consensus.

 Nevertheless, according to Sedlmeir and colleagues (2020), even with these alternatives, "we should expect that there will still be tens of thousands of nodes". Such networks will have negligible power consumption compared to Bitcoin, but remaining "high compared to a centralized non-blockchain system, with minimal redundancy (induced by backups)". What's more, we still don't know (in 2022) whether proof-of-stake will not also encourage the risk of centralization (observed with manage pools in proof-of-work; in Bitcoin and Ethereum, "around three pools are enough to coordinate a 51% attack (4 in Bitcoin, 3 in Ethereum at the time of this calculation). In a proof-of-stake system, if we assume 30% participation, including all exchanges, then three exchanges would suffice to make a 51% attack; if participation rises to 40%, the number required rises to eight. However, exchanges won't be able to participate with all their ethers; because they have to take withdrawals into account." According to the Ethereum FAQ: "Centralization is less harmful in proof-of-stake than in proof-of-work, as there are much cheaper ways to recover from successful 51% attacks; there's no need to switch to a new mining algorithm". In all cases, however, sharding always implies an intensity of transaction verification workload proportional to the amount of capital invested, and therefore increasing energy consumption.

- another way would be to force (by political, regulatory and fiscal means) blockchain technology to "decarbonize" (by evolving towards a *low-carbon blockchain technology* and/or by paying off its negative externalities for the environment; this poses new challenges, to regulators on the one hand and to digital currency computer scientists on the other. One way forward proposed by Jon Truby is to subsidize or reward carbon-neutral or carbon-negative blockchains, and tax "dirty" blockchains, following the model of carbon finance (whose track record is disputed). In 2022, noting that "many popular types of blockchain have resisted pressure to reduce their environmental impact, including Bitcoin, whose attributed annual emissions in 2021 will produce emissions responsible for around 19,000 future deaths" a team of researchers proposed to more clearly "link the damage caused by proof-of-work blockchains to climate change and human mortality" to incentivize the evolution of blockchain consensus protocols and promote the energy efficiency of miners to mitigate the environmental damage they create.

Howson and de Vries (2022) suggest, "as a matter of urgency (...) to reduce the threat of catastrophic climate change and to help the poorest develop sustainably", without expecting "win-win outcomes for all", 4 regulatory paths:

1.) promote voluntary commitments by the private sector to use only renewable energies;

2.) to encourage voluntary carbon offsetting;

3.) use existing financial regulations and tax frameworks ;

4.) impose national and/or international bans on crypto-currency "mining";

Others (example(s) to come in 2022) propose indicating to the general public and investors an ethical or environmental rating, for example for each crypto-currency, which has some new implications for crypto-currency literature.

The designer of bitcoin wanted it to be resistant to high-frequency trading: the architecture of its blockchain and its mining protocol mean that a bitcoin transaction cannot be validated in less than 10 minutes (approximately). The disadvantage of this necessary delay is that scalability is mechanically limited; in other words, the system cannot adapt to a change in the order of magnitude of demand, yet it could be faced with an exponential demand for transactions.

Bitcoiners have circumvented this limitation of the Bitcoin protocol by creating a *Lightning Network*. In this "layer", which is largely external to Bitcoin, and in complete confidentiality (no individual payment details from the *Lightning* Network are recorded publicly on the blockchain), they escape blockchain transactions, while benefiting from lower routing fees payable to the network's intermediate nodes. And, unlike the Bitcoin blockchain, the Lightning Network protocol imposes no intrinsic limit on transaction throughput (in other words, the number of payments per second); this is limited only by the capacity and speed of each node. Finally, on the Lightning Network, it takes less than a minute to settle a transaction, and often only a few milliseconds. On the other hand, they lose out in terms of security, and must all participate in a "watchtower" system designed to detect and block fraudsters.

How it works

Proof of work, a historic consensus-building method

Blockchain is a form of implementation of the "Byzantine Generals Problem". This mathematical problem involves ensuring that a set of computer components working in concert can cope with failures (or malfunctions) and produce a consensus. The system must be able to maintain its reliability in the event that some of the participants send erroneous or malicious information, as in the case of a cryptocurrency, to bypass the double-spending verification by the network's miners (double-spending consists of making two payments simultaneously: one to oneself and another to a victim; the aim is to have the payment to the victim registered in the blockchain long enough to deceive the victim, but registered in such a way that it is eventually entirely replaced by the payment to oneself).

The historical method for achieving this type of consensus is "*proof* of *work*". This method uses a mathematical problem, the solution to which verifies that the "miner" has indeed done a job. The protocol uses a cryptographic system based on a decentralized proof system: solving the proof requires a high level of computing power, provided by the miners. Miners are entities whose role is to supply the network with computing power, to enable updating of the decentralized database. For this update, miners must confirm new blocks by validating the data. In the case of bitcoin, when adding blocks to the chain, a brute-force cryptographic problem must be solved before a new block can be added. Depending on the "difficulty" of the chain at the time of resolution, this may require the same operation to be repeated several hundred billion times. In the case of bitcoin, a miner is only remunerated for his work if he is the first to solve the cryptographic problem.

There is competition between miners to add new blocks, but also a certain solidarity. Anyone can lend their computing power to mine, but the more miners there are, the higher the "difficulty" and the harder it is to solve the cryptographic problem. Conversely, if miners stop mining, the difficulty decreases. The protocol can become virtually unbreakable when no single group of miners becomes the majority (thus preventing the 51% attack).

Among the pitfalls associated with this method are the latency required to validate a transaction, and the decreasing profitability of miners. The high energy consumption associated with this method is also pointed out. Faced with these facts, the blockchain community is debating the use of consensus methods that would no longer be proof-of-work, but, for example, proof-of-participation.

Other consensus methods

Several entities use other consensus methods. For example, the Peercoin cryptocurrency uses a mixture of "*proof of work*" and "*proof of stake*", i.e. it adapts the difficulty of the work according to the "share" of each node. Participation" is defined as the product of the number of peercoins held and the age of each node. The higher the participation, the lower the difficulty of the hash function (hashing is a cryptographic process used to reduce a set of data. It governs the *proof-of-work* system. *Hashes* are simple to verify but very difficult to solve); this mechanically reduces the energy consumption of the mining algorithms (SCRYPT or SHA-256) needed to create money.

Ethereum, which used the "proof of work" method, finally migrated to proof of participation in 2022.

Burstcoin, on the other hand, uses *proof* of *capacity* (PoC), where hard disks store "traces", whose presence is proven by accessing them. This protocol is distinguished by its low power consumption.

Governance

It's important to note that the notion of *Law* in blockchains should not be understood in the sense of legislative laws (passed by a nation's parliament, for example), but of a law *internal to* the blockchain process, managed by the governance of that blockchain. The common phrase *Code is law,* regularly used as a rule of blockchain governance, therefore does not refer to national or international laws, but only to the "rules of governance" enacted and applicable to the blockchain. In this case, these laws are often no more than computer codes and algorithms, so that the rules enacted can be verified by miners during transaction verification sessions. Any transaction that complies with the codes is accepted into the blockchain; otherwise, the modification is rejected, without any human intervention on the part of the governance (with a few exceptions).

There are several possible modes of governance:

- An "open" mode (anyone can read and write the chain registers). In this case, as a general rule, the law applicable to the chain is the law (algorithmic code) designated by the parties.

- A "semi-closed" mode (only a central organization can write, but read access is freer). This can be used for functions assigned to governments (cadastres, etc.) or to institutions managing secure data (food traceability, etc.). In this case, the rules are freer, with the central body having control over the technical aspects of blockchain validation.

- a closed mode (only a central organization can write, no one can read except that organization). In this case, the interest lies in the theoretical robustness and traceability of the process, which doesn't need to be (or shouldn't be) public, but which does need this security. Note that in this case, it remains vulnerable to a 51% attack, due to its non-decentralized, non-public nature.

Open governance does not, however, mean an absence of governance. In the case of Bitcoin, which accounts for 50% of the total value of crypto-currencies in circulation as of August 18, 2018, governance is provided by the community, in a decentralized manner. Decentralization is a major contribution of blockchain and, by ricochet, of crypto-currencies. There's a wiki (opened in 2010, containing more than 1,500 pages as of August 18, 2018), IRC discussion forums devoted to governance, technique, etc., and even an emergency protocol in the event of a proven hack or bug. Of course, what's available for Bitcoin isn't necessarily available or applicable for other cryptocurrencies, especially the newer and/or more confidential ones.

Organization

Management science researchers are investigating the role of blockchains in supporting different forms of collaboration. Blockchains can support both cooperation (i.e. the prevention of opportunistic behavior) and coordination (i.e. communication and information sharing). Thanks to the reliability, transparency, traceability of records and immutability of information, blockchains facilitate collaboration in a way that differs from both the traditional use of contracts and relational norms. Unlike contracts, blockchains do not rely directly on the legal system to enforce agreements. Furthermore, unlike the use of relational norms, blockchains do not require trust or direct relationships between collaborators.

Transactions

In the world of blockchains, a "transaction" is any operation that modifies the state of the blockchain, and therefore adds new data that it will store irreversibly. Transactions can be :

- exchanges between users (user A sends x tokens to user B);

- execution of operations by a *smart contract* (e.g. execution of a smart contract on the Ethereum blockchain), at the request of a user or another *smart contract*.

Originally, with the Bitcoin network, transactions were only of the first type, since it was only possible to send a quantity of "bitcoin" tokens to another address. The term "transaction" now has a much broader meaning, closer to the concept of a computer transaction, which involves interacting with a database (to write, modify or read data).

Blocks

The various transactions recorded are grouped together in blocks. After recording recent transactions, a new block is generated and all transactions are validated by the miners, who analyze the entire history of the blockchain. If the block is valid, it is time-stamped and added to the blockchain. The transactions it contains are then visible throughout the network. Once added to the chain, a block can no longer be modified or deleted (theoretically), guaranteeing the network's authenticity and security.

Each block in the chain consists of the following elements:

- several transactions ;

- a checksum (*"hash"),* used as an identifier ;

- the checksum of the previous block (with the exception of the first block in the chain, called the genesis block);

- a measure of the amount of work required to produce the block. This is defined by the consensus method used within the blockchain, such as "proof of work", or "proof of participation".

Addresses

In a blockchain, each user owns a wallet, represented by a public address (a "public key"). This can be compared to the address of a bank account, which allows anyone to send funds to it via a bank transfer.

The owner of an address can manipulate it through the use of his private key, itself generally derived from a mnemonic phrase (a sequence of several words, also known as a "*seed phrase*", depending on the algorithm used).

For example, on the Ethereum blockchain, the address "0x8F3e32453A32C412D2ff51C3b4A25Db618469842" can be manipulated by its owner using the following seed phrase: *crime guard diary maple around goat prepare affair equip gun wasp evidence*, or the private key "0xef1a0ca2d3de28e2945f76eb314d90d564e3bb232f833 bbe846629e5e6856c73".

Applications

Cryptocurrency

The flagship application of this technology is that of cryptocurrencies such as bitcoin, which is far from being the only virtual currency: there are many others, such as Ether, Monero, and thousands of others of varying degrees of confidentiality.

In terms of participatory financing, these crypto-currencies have enabled the establishment of ICOs (*Initial Coin Offering*), which enable extremely rapid fund-raising.

Possible applications

Beyond its monetary aspect, this information storage technology could have multiple applications (provided a secure consensus algorithm that does not use cryptocurrency is found), such as :

- Applications using smart contracts to exchange all kinds of goods and services;

- Ways to reduce payment and transaction costs. International banks made announcements in 2015 on these subjects. Twenty-five of them, for example, signed a partnership with a US company R3 for the use of *blockchains* in financial markets. Citibank also announced its desire to issue its own cryptocurrency, the Citicoin. Similarly, in April 2015, UBS bank opened its own research laboratory in London dedicated to the study of blockchain technology and its applications in the financial sector. Through such research and consortia, banks hope to establish a blockchain-based technology that will become a benchmark within the banking field. Indeed, the consortium or bank that succeeds in bringing out a proven technology first will be able to charge other players in the financial sector for its own service;

- ○ Blockchain-based automotive EDI system: described by Rahul Guhathakurta in "The Age of Blockchain", the concept of a Blockchain-based automotive EDI system aims to improve supply chain transparency and combat fraud and counterfeiting. The combination of EDI and Blockchain enables an authenticated relationship between the automaker, the OEM (Original Equipment Manufacturer) and the car dealer. Each EDI transaction (ASN or DESADV) verifies in a Blockchain the authenticity of the OEMs shipped.

- ○ BtoB EDI communication sharing solution: Among the work presented to FIATA (International Federation of Freight Forwarders Associations) in 2019, a Blockchain-powered EDI data sharing platform. The EDI message is no longer transmitted point-to-point, but to a network of authenticated partners included in a Blockchain. This solution enables immediate and simultaneous distribution of secure, truthful information to all authorized third parties. In international trade, forwarding agents, logisticians, carriers, insurers, customs, exporters and importers all share the same authenticated information. This speeds up and secures the financial transactions linked to the operation.

- o GS1 standardization work: To facilitate the adoption of Blockchain by companies and the sharing of stored information, product catalogs, traceability of product origins, logistics events, GS1 is working to promote GS1, ISO, EPCIS (Electronic Product Code Information Services) standards to the Blockchain community.

- Ways of improving their predictive systems, known as "oracles", for insurance companies in particular;

- The development of *peer-to-peer* insurance ;

- Food chain product traceability: In 2018, Carrefour in collaboration with IBM, launched 'transparent chicken' from Auvergne with a blockchain system that detailed the entire supply chain.

- Luxury product traceability: In 2021, LVMH is launching *Aura Blockchain Consortium*, a project with the aim of guaranteeing product certification, ensuring authenticity and traceability for customers and partner brands. This technology combines a product identifier with a customer identifier, to help combat counterfeit products.

Administration

The technology is being developed in Ghana by the NGO Bitland to create a virtual land registry. A similar project was envisaged for a time in Honduras, but ultimately came to nothing. Georgia has also announced a blockchain cadastre experiment in partnership with Bitcoin start-up BitFury, as has Sweden with start-up ChromaWay.

Industrial group General Electric has chosen to invest in a start-up called Xage, which leverages blockchain to create digital footprints of industrial machines, thereby identifying and securing every machine on a power grid.

In Europe, blockchain technology is being considered for notary, diploma management and digital identity applications.

Identification and possible drifts

Even in the early years, experts warned against the possible overuse of blockchains. For example, in 2018, the National Institute of Standards and Technology (USA) presented a report indicating that many problems remain better solved with databases or simple emails.

The blockchain system is also being used to offer a privacy-preserving information storage system that places information in the "hands of users" rather than a third party, and to bypass the censorship of centralized systems such as Google/ Youtube. For example, the brave browsers co-founded by Brendan Eich or dissenter, or the Verasity video platform.

Blockchain technology can be used to combat the counterfeiting of physical goods, as in the traceability of bottles of wine, or to identify individuals.

Cryptocurrency

A **cryptocurrency**, also known as a **cryptoasset**, **cryptocurrency**, **cryptocurrency** or **cybercurrency, is** an electronic currency (digital asset) issued peer-to-peer, without the need for a bank or central bank, that can be used via a decentralized computer network.

First introduced in 2009 with blockchain, cryptoassets use cryptographic technologies and enable transaction issuance and settlement processes that no longer involve a human intermediary. However, they are sometimes dependent on a blockchain system that consumes considerable computing and energy resources, and are susceptible to high price volatility.

The best-known cryptocurrencies are Bitcoin (BTC) and Ethereum (ETH).

Trends and statistics

As of April 26, 2023, according to *CoinMarketCap*, there are 23,642 cryptoassets, or cryptocurrencies, worth €1,079.1 billion. In 2023, 46 million Americans would hold Bitcoins.

Prevalence: according to statista, in April 2023 Africa, Asia and South America had the highest number of people claiming to have crypto-currencies (most often Bitcoin); and more specifically, Nigeria and Turkey had the highest proportion of the general population holding crypto-currencies (47% of respondents in both cases).

According to a TripleA survey, in 2022, around 5% of French people (often men, rather well-educated and among the country's wealthiest, and half aged between 18 and 34) held cryptocurrencies (compared with 3.3% in 2021), with Bitcoin being the most common (72, 83% of cases), ahead of Ethereum (28.9%).

Operating principles

A cryptocurrency is based on a blockchain distributed in a decentralized registry and encrypted according to a computer protocol.

Blockchain

A cryptocurrency is based on a blockchain, a distributed ledger (or general ledger) that can be consulted by anyone, and which records all the network's actions from the outset. The information to be added is called transactions, and is grouped into blocks. A transaction may, for example, be a transfer of cryptocurrency from one logical address, held in an address wallet, to another.

Network participants, known as nodes, own, store and verify their own versions of the chain, from the very first block (known as the genesis block). A blockchain is considered valid when it can be fully verified starting from the genesis block. As there is no central authority or trusted third party, the system is said to be decentralized. To guarantee the immutability of the chain, i.e. that no modification has been made to an old block, the blocks are chained together using cryptographic hash functions.

Each node is actually a computer connected to the network via the Internet. The system does not operate in real time, as there can be significant latency when sending or receiving transactions and blocks across the network. Where different versions of the same string exist, the rule is to choose the longest valid string.

Consensus and block generation

In order to ensure that all the players in the distributed network agree on the same version of the chain and synchronize themselves, a solution must be found to the problem of consensus. The aim of consensus is to designate the entity responsible for proposing a new block to the network, while ensuring that the creation of new units of currency is gradual. Most cryptocurrencies have a cap (i.e. a maximum quantity) on the money supply that will eventually be in circulation. This cap is designed to mimic the scarcity (and value) of precious metals and avoid hyperinflation.

Once a block has been created and validated, each node involved in its creation is allocated an amount of cryptocurrency, in proportion to its effort. Participation in money creation, known as "mining", follows a logarithmic pattern that aims to reproduce the discovery of gold (or other precious metals):

- At first, few people are looking for gold, so finding it is relatively straightforward.

- Then, as information spreads and more and more people search, gold becomes harder and harder to find and rarer and rarer.

- As a result, players are investing more and more, pushing back the limits and forcing smaller researchers to give up.

- Because the resource is exhaustible and increasingly costly to obtain, its value increases, while its chance of discovery decreases.

This election can be made in different ways, depending on the nature of the blockchain. Proof-of-work is the original method used by bitcoin, when it was created in 2009, but work is underway to propose new ones.

Proof of work

The proof of work consists of a participant solving a complex cryptographic problem, thereby assuring the other members of the network that a substantial computational effort has been made on his or her part. While solving this problem requires time and resources, the proposed solution must be easily verifiable.

The problem to be solved is deduced directly from the blockchain (for example, from the content of the current block in the case of bitcoin). The difficulty is adapted to the computing power of the network, so that the creation of new blocks respects a constant average frequency.

Although in theory simple CPUs or GPUs (graphics card processors) are sufficient to solve a cryptographic problem, today's best-known blockchains (bitcoin, ethereum, etc.) involve a level of difficulty too high to be achievable in an acceptable timeframe. Participating in the computation of cryptocurrency transactions therefore now requires a significant investment, since it is essential to use specialized systems such as FPGAs or ASICs. There are, however, other cryptocurrencies which are less attractive at the moment, because they are new or based on different algorithms, enabling less powerful systems to take part in the calculation.

In the case of proofs of work, a flaw allows the corruption of consensus properties by a group holding the equivalent of 51% of the computing power. This flaw has been dubbed the 51% attack.

Block generation raises the question of the energy expended to create cryptocurrency (see Proof of work power consumption).

Proof of stake

To enable less energy-intensive cryptocurrency production, in September 2022 Ethereum made a transition from its proof-of-work validation method to proof-of-stake. This choice comes after lengthy debate and several years of research by Ethereum founder Vitalik Buterin and developer Vlad Zamfir. To participate in the validation of transactions and the creation of blocks, users must place part of their capital in escrow. Users are rewarded for the temporary unavailability of their Ethereum by receiving the currency created simultaneously with the new block. The Ethereum protocol requires 32 ethers in escrow to participate in block validation. In September 2022, an ether is worth 1,578 euros, so the minimum stake will be around 50,000 euros.

History

Terminology

In "cryptocurrency", the prefix "*crypto*" (from the ancient Greek kruptos (κρυπτός): "hidden") refers to the systematic use of cryptography to encode information.

Institutions such as the G20 Finance Ministers and the Banque de France refute the term "cryptocurrency", considering that "cryptocurrencies" do not fulfill the functions of a currency. They use the term "crypto-asset".

In France, the term "crypto-asset" refers to "virtual assets stored on an electronic medium enabling a community of users accepting them as payment to carry out transactions without having to resort to legal tender."

Since January 1, 2019, the legal and tax term enshrined in law is digital asset, which technically contains "cryptocurrencies".

In the past, other terms have been used successively by various regulatory authorities (see *below*).

1998-2009: origins and confidential distribution

The concept of cryptocurrency was around long before Bitcoin was created. DigiCash Inc. was founded in 1989 by David Chaum, with the aim of creating the world's first virtual currency. DigiCash was a virtual currency company. It created an anonymous payment protocol based on cryptography. However, Digicash failed to achieve mass adoption of its cryptocurrency. The company was forced to declare bankruptcy in 1998.

In 1998, Wei Dai published a description of "b-money", an anonymous electronic cash system. Shortly afterwards,

Nick Szabo created "Bit Gold", which required users to complete a proof-of-work function whose solutions were encrypted, put together and published. Bitcoin, created in 2009 by a developer (or group of developers) using the pseudonym Satoshi Nakamoto, exploits the SHA-256 algorithm as a proof-of-work system.Other crypto-currencies are being proposed, such as Litecoin (which uses scrypt as proof of work and relies on faster transaction confirmations), Peercoin (which uses a hybrid proof-of-work system and has an annual inflation rate of 1%) and Namecoin (which serves as a decentralized DNS, making internet censorship more difficult).Several other crypto-currencies have been created: not all have been successful, particularly those bringing little innovation.

2011-2017: public adoption of three generations of cryptocurrencies

After their appearance, cryptocurrencies gained media and public attention. Since 2011, this interest has increased, particularly during the rapid rise in the Bitcoin price (April 2013). From 2014 onwards, a second generation of cryptocurrencies appeared, such as Monero, Ethereum and Nxt with new features such as stealth addresses, so-called *"smart"* contracts, the use of side blockchains or backed by physical assets such as gold. Representatives of several central banks have stated that the use of cryptocurrencies poses significant challenges to economic equilibria. In particular, from the point of view of the price of credit. For Gareth Murphy (US Central Bank), "widespread use [of crypto-currencies] would make it more difficult for statistical agencies to collect data on economic activity, which is in turn used by governments to guide the economy"; crypto-currencies are a new challenge for central banks' monetary and exchange rate policy management.

1, 2 and 3 generation cryptocurrencies:

1. The first generation is represented by Bitcoin (2009). Solidly established and the originator of the cryptocurrency media craze, it suffers from a number of shortcomings that are regularly pointed out, including its slowness and relatively

small block size. Moreover, Bitcoin mining consumes a great deal of energy and computing resources, generating heavy ecological, water and carbon footprints (according to a Selectra study, at the time of the study, Bitcoin had a growing energy and carbon footprint, and was already at least equivalent to that of Norway. A recent (2022) LCA study of bitcoin mining in the top 10 mining countries (*China, USA, Kazakhstan, Russia, Iran, Malaysia, Canada, Germany, Ireland, Norway*) showed that with a 53.3% share of global mining, China had the most negative environmental impact, including in terms of marine ecotoxicity and on human health with 0.0043 DALY, and that with an equal share of mining, Germany and Kazakhstan had the most negative environmental impacts). While China has finally banned mining at home, it has gained strength in Russia, the USA/Texas and Kazakhstan... contributing even more than other cryptocurrencies to the general degradation of the environment, and to the detriment of human health. In 2018, Mora & al. in Nature were already wondering whether the exponential aspect of Bitcoin's energy needs, on its own, might not lead humanity to exceed the +2°C climate threshold .

2. A second generation (2011) features either minor improvements or technological innovations enabling new functions. The archetype of this second generation is Ethereum (derived from Bitcoin's source code), which makes use of smart contracts.

3. The third generation (since 2017): noting new limitations, notably in terms of capacity, security and governance, new cryptocurrencies have emerged, such as EOS.IO, Cardano (ADA), AION, ICON (ICX) and Raiden Network (RDN), for the best-known. EOS.IO is itself derived from Ethereum. They all bring innovations to the table, but as of August 2018, none has taken the lead over the others.

The first stablecoin ("stable cryptocurrency"), bitUSD, was introduced in 2014. The launch of cryptocurrencies with a fixed price is based on the advantages claimed by this type of currency (greater consumer confidence in a currency with a fixed price and less speculation, or nationals of countries where the monetary instability of the system leads to restrictions on the control of their capital).

The founder of Robocoin launched the first bitcoin ATM in the USA on February 20, 2014 in Austin, Texas. Similar to an ATM, it also features an ID card scanner.

In 2018, the market is down compared to its 2017 year-end. but the number of job offers in the sector continues to rise.

On August 21, 2019, employees of the South Ukraine nuclear power plant who connected it to the internet to mine cryptocurrency were arrested by the secret service.

At the end of 2019 there were nearly 2,400 cryptocurrencies on the coinmarketcap website.

2020s: a shrinking, unstable market

In 2020, with its price having more than doubled since the beginning of the year, Bitcoin is attracting young savers, along with other crypto-currencies, but this market is proving to be particularly volatile, marked by sharp and unexpected depreciations, including a sudden collapse in January 2022, This followed a halving of Bitcoin's value in three months (from over $69,000 in November 2021 to $36,000 on January 24, 2022, then to $16,000 on November 20, 2022, a drop of almost 75%, according to some analysts, in response to the Fed's monetary strategies.

Excluding Bitcoin, as of May 9, 2021, according to *CoinMarketCap*, there are 5,022 cryptoassets, or cryptocurrencies, with an estimated value of 2,031 billion euros. A growing number of cryptoactives are in circulation, but Bitcoin remains in first place (876.6 billion euros), ahead of Ethereum (410.5 billion euros). Between them, they account for almost two-thirds of the market's total value. The majority of Europeans want cryptocurrencies to be regulated; a minority buy them in the hope of enriching themselves or for personal gain.

Emerging countries are increasingly adopting cryptocurrencies as a means of combating inflation, devaluation of national currencies or over-reliance on the dollar.

In February 2022, the Financial Stability Board (FSB), supervisor of global finance, warned of the growing role taken by "stablecoins" and decentralized finance (DeFi), as well as the growing links between cryptoactives and speculative finance; the cryptocurrency market ($2,600 billion) remains limited compared to the rest of the financial system, with around 1% of global financial assets, but its growth is such (3.5-fold increase in size by 2021) that it raises fears of a financial bubble. FSB Chairman Klaas Knot, Governor of the Dutch Central Bank, also denounces "misleading designations": "most 'stablecoins' are neither stable nor currencies", and finance claiming to be *decentralized* is paradoxically "often quite centralized" via the technologies used or intermediation platforms.

In 2022, the loss of parity led to a loss of confidence and a significant fall in the Terra stablecoin. This steered the global cryptocurrency market lower, wiping out over

US$250 billion in the space of two years. The value of Luna's Terra crypto asset falls by around 90%, rendering cryptocurrency tokens now almost worthless. For Janet Yellen, US Secretary of the Treasury, the episode "simply illustrates that this is a fast-growing product, that it poses risks to financial stability, and that we need the right framework". Janet Yellen, who is a former chairwoman of the Board of Governors of the US Federal Reserve (FED), is calling for regulation covering crypto-currencies and digital asset trading, broaching the subject for the first time in a landmark speech.

November sees the collapse of FTX, one of the leading centralized cryptocurrency exchange platforms, with the revelation of highly risky and unsustainable borrowing and lending by the company and related investment funds. The price of bitcoin plunges below $17,000 for the first time since 2020. Against this backdrop, economist Nouriel Roubini describes cryptocurrencies and some of their key players as a "totally corrupt ecosystem".

In March 2023, European police agency Europol and the US Department of Justice announced that crypto-currency mixer ChipMixer had been seized, alleging that it was helping to mask "the digital money trail for online drug traffickers, Russian military hackers and North Korean cybercriminals". The Ministry of Justice said it had charged Vietnamese national Minh Quoc Nguyen, with money laundering and identity theft in connection with the operation of the platform. ChipMixer is a mixer set up in mid-2017, specializing in mixing or removing leads linked to virtual currency assets. According to Europol, it is "one of the largest crypto-currency laundries on the dark web". More than 40 million euros ($42.2 million) worth of crypto-currency was seized. Digital currency tracking service Elliptic considers that ChipMixer was used to launder more than $844 million in Bitcoin that was directly linked to illicit activities - including at least $666 million from crypto-currency thefts.

Stable cryptocurrencies (*stablecoins*)

Stable cryptocurrencies (*stablecoins*) aim to replicate the value of an asset, such as the dollar, gold or the euro. The aim is to avoid being subject to market volatility.

Notable stable cryptocurrencies include:

- USDT (Tether)
- DAI
- USDC (Coinbase)
- EURL (Lugh)
- EUROC

Stable cryptocurrencies are seen by central banks as potentially affecting financial stability, but also undermining monetary sovereignty. The Financial Stability Forum is proposing that stable cryptocurrencies should be supervised and regulated, at least those which, due to their global and universal nature, pose a problem in terms of financial risks. This recommendation follows on from the G7's position in 2019.

Basel Committee rules require banks to assign "risk weights" to the different types of assets they hold in order to determine capital requirements. Stablecoins would fall under the existing rules and be treated in the same way as bonds, loans, deposits, equities or commodities.

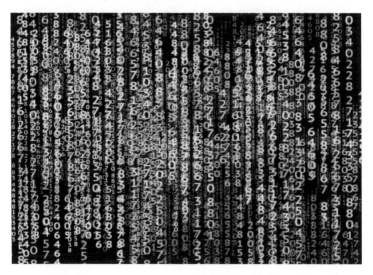

Fund raising

A fundraiser can be used to create a cryptocurrency. This type of activity can be regulated.

An "initial *coin offering*" (ICO) is a form of financing, halfway between fundraising and equity crowdfunding, through the pre-sale of a new cryptocurrency. The first notable Initial coin offering was that of Ethereum in 2014.

In 2017, this market is still poorly regulated, so in September China banned ICOs on its territory. In Russia, Vladimir Putin approves the use of ICOs, demanding that appropriate regulations be put in place to control the cryptocurrency market. According to South Korea's financial watchdog, it will be illegal to issue digital tokens to raise funds.

A *Security Token Offering* or STO is an *Initial Coin Offering* governed by legal standards.

In France, in September 2017, Domraider became the first French company to practice fundraising by this means, through its cryptocurrency, the DRT (DomRaider token). The Clermont-Ferrand-based start-up is raising 56 million euros to create a decentralized platform dedicated to real-time auctions on the blockchain. DRTs serve as a means of payment on the auction blockchain and are exchangeable on cryptocurrency marketplaces.

Legal framework in France

The legal framework applicable to crypto-currencies requires them to be given a legal status: a distinction must be made between legal tender, electronic money and, finally, the new category of digital asset, the latter notion corresponding to crypto-currencies. The European Central Bank's digital euro project does not involve the creation of a cryptocurrency, but rather the digitization of the legal tender that is the euro.

In France, cryptocurrencies have been defined and regulated by law since January 1, 2019. After a period of relative uncertainty, they are now part of the broader category of digital assets, and their tax regime is defined and clarified by the Directorate General of Public Finances.

The desire of private companies like Facebook or Telegram to launch a cryptocurrency is also raising concerns among states. Their danger was discussed at the G7 Finance summit in 2019. At the time, US Treasury Secretary Steven Mnuchin reported "very serious concerns about Libra, which can be misused to launder money or fund terrorism". The member countries' finance ministers then agreed to make rapid progress on the issue.

Following the publication of a report on October 2, 2020, the European Central Bank has indicated that it is launching a consultation on the creation of a "digital euro". This would consist of a virtual currency "different" from cryptocurrencies, the latter being considered destined to be highly volatile and risky since they are not backed by a Central Bank.

As for cryptocurrency exchange platforms, they must be registered with the Autorité des Marchés Financiers

(AMF) as Prestataire de Service sur Actifs Numériques (PSAN). French platform Coinhouse was the first to obtain this status on March 17, 2020. Binance received authorization from the Autorité des Marchés Financiers to operate its crypto-currency exchange platform in France on May 4, 2022. France becomes the first major European country to approve the site.

Legal qualification

Article L. 111-1 of the French Monetary and Financial Code establishes the principle that the legal tender in France is the euro: a merchant may refuse a payment in Bitcoin, but not a payment in euros.

Article L. 315-1 of the French Monetary and Financial Code defines electronic money as "monetary value stored in electronic form, including magnetic form, representing a claim on the issuer, which is issued against the remittance of funds for the purposes of payment transactions as defined in Article L. 133-3, and which is accepted by a natural or legal person other than the issuer of electronic money". A "cryptocurrency" such as Bitcoin, which does not represent a claim on the issuer, is therefore not an electronic money, as defined by European legislation, transposed in France in the Monetary and Financial Code.

Article L. 54-10-1 of the French Monetary and Financial Code defines digital assets, which include cryptocurrencies, as "any digital representation of value which is not issued or guaranteed by a central bank or public authority, which is not necessarily attached to a legal tender and which does not have the legal status of a currency, but which is accepted by natural or legal persons as a means of exchange and which can be transferred, stored or exchanged electronically". However, it does not define "cryptocurrencies".

Article L. 552-2 of the French Monetary and Financial Code defines a digital token as "any intangible asset representing, in digital form, one or more rights that can be issued, registered, stored or transferred by means of a shared electronic recording device enabling the owner of said asset to be identified, directly or indirectly".

The legal qualification of "currency" claimed by the promoters of "crypto-currencies" is contested by governments and central banks, who default to the notion of asset, subject to the same fluctuations and risks (and potentially taxation) as other non-monetary financial assets. The term "crypto-asset" is therefore recommended by the Banque de France and the G20 finance ministers, as "crypto-assets do not perform the key functions of a virtual currency" (*Banque de France Focus*, n 16, March 5, 2018). The Court of Cassation, indirectly, has qualified bitcoin as a "virtual currency" (Court of Cassation, Criminal Division, February 20, 2019, n 18-86.951).

Crypto-currencies are beyond the control of the state, but affect the economy, which is itself the subject of public policy: they cannot be included in monetary policy. What's more, their pseudonymity (anonymity for some, such as Monero, Dash, Zerocoin, or when they are laundered via a crypto-currency blender) makes illicit transactions just as possible as cash. Through various regulations, they are monitored by monetary authorities along two axes:

- control the legality of goods or services purchased using cryptocurrencies and thus avoid illicit purchases,

- monitor conversion into legal tender and thus detect money laundering.

Cryptocurrency and debt security

Article L.54-10-1 of the French Monetary and Financial Code specifies in 1° that digital assets also include digital tokens, "to the exclusion of those fulfilling the characteristics of the financial instruments mentioned in Article L. 211-1 (which include debt securities) and the savings bonds mentioned in Article L. 223-1".

Applicable tax regime

Cryptocurrencies went through a relative period of legal uncertainty before the legislator intervened as part of the vote on the 2019 Finance Act.

The first regime comes into force with the tax instruction of July 11, 2014: cryptocurrencies are then qualified as "virtual units of account stored on an electronic medium", taxable on the progressive scale of income tax, in the category of non-commercial profits (or industrial and commercial profits, in the case of habitual activity).

The second regime comes into force with the ruling handed down by the Conseil d'Etat on April 26, 2018 (8 and 3 chambers, n 417809): cryptocurrencies are qualified as "intangible movable property" within the meaning of civil property law, taxable in the category of capital gains on movable property falling under Article 150 UA of the CGI, or failing that as non-commercial profits (for mining activities) or industrial and commercial profits (for trading, on a regular basis). In addition to social security contributions, a flat rate of 12.9% (article 200A of the CGI) was applied to the capital gain, which was also exempt from taxation for all sales (resale value, not capital gain value) of less than €5,000.

The current regime, voted in with the Finance Act of December 28, 2018, defines cryptocurrencies as digital assets in Article L. 54-10-1 of the French Monetary and Financial Code: digital assets are civilly intangible movable property, taxable for income tax purposes, based on Article 150 VH bis of the French General Tax Code. Capital gains on the sale of digital assets are subject to the same flat-rate withholding tax as income from movable assets: a flat rate of 12.8%, plus 17.2% social security contributions (total flat tax of 30%). A tax exemption applies when the gross annual amount of sales (not capital gains) is less than €305.

Declaration of accounts held on a platform

As of January 1, 2020, any account opened, held or closed on a digital asset exchange platform or intermediary must be declared at the same time as the taxpayer completes his or her income tax return: the taxpayer must complete the 3916 bis form, which is different from the 3916 form for traditional foreign bank accounts.

Role of the Autorité des marchés financiers

In France, the Autorité des marchés financiers (AMF) has had its powers extended by French and European legislation. From 2024-2025, capital guarantees and a liability insurance policy to compensate customers where applicable will be expected.

Legal framework in other countries

Sovereign cryptocurrencies

- In late 2017, Venezuelan President Nicolas Maduro created a cryptocurrency, petro, anchored to the price of a barrel of oil, with the aim of circumventing US sanctions. It disappears in January 2024.

- In January 2018, the Bank of England announced that it wished to create a cryptocurrency indexed to the British currency.

- In Canada and Singapore, institutions are also considering developing official cryptocurrency payment systems.

- In 2018, the Marshall Islands became the first country in the world to launch a legal cryptocurrency.

- In 2018, Turkey is also planning its own currency, the Turkcoin, to boost the economy.

- In 2018, Iran is considering creating a national cryptocurrency, based on bitcoin, to counter the fall in the national currency due to the return of US sanctions.

- In 2021, the People's Republic of China is declaring all cryptocurrency transactions illegal, and plans to launch its digital currency to do away with cash in 2022, having initiated the movement in 2014 and filed 80 patents. It's called DCEP or Digital Currency Electronic Payment.

Bans

Some countries prohibit the use and marketing of cryptocurrencies, According to the U.S. Library of Congress, we can distinguish.

- an absolute ban on crypto-currencies: Algeria, Bolivia, Egypt, Iraq, Morocco, Nepal, Pakistan, United Arab Emirates, Vietnam.

- an implicit ban on crypto-currencies where legislation makes it difficult to access crypto-currency markets: Bahrain, Bangladesh, China, Colombia, Dominican Republic, Indonesia, Iran, Kuwait, Lesotho, Lithuania, Macau, Oman, Qatar, Saudi Arabia, Taiwan, Thailand

For example:

- Bangladesh, in late 2017, reaffirmed that crypto-currencies are non-compliant with various laws. Every user risks prosecution.

- In Pakistan, the Central Bank has made crypto-currency transactions illegal. Anyone investing in or owning crypto-currencies risks prosecution.

- In Uzbekistan, as of December 6, 2019, buying crypto-currencies is considered illegal.

- In Qatar, at the end of December 2019, the Qatar Financial Center (QFC) made crypto-currencies illegal, whether trading, issuing, storing or transferring crypto-assets.

- In Algeria, since the 2018 Finance Law, the purchase, sale, use or possession of crypto-currency has been prohibited.

- In Morocco, anyone involved in transactions with crypto-currencies risks a fine or arrest

- In Burundi, as of September 2019, crypto-currencies are illegal.

- In Bolivia, crypto-currencies are illegal. Users risk a fine or arrest.

- In Ecuador, in 2014, crypto-currencies were banned by Parliament.

- In September 2017, Chinese regulators announced a ban on initial coin offerings (ICOs).

- In February 2021, the Nigerian Central Bank (CBN) reminds us that the use of cryptocurrencies has been illegal since 2017. It asks commercial banks to "identify individuals and entities" with cryptocurrency accounts, in order to "close them immediately". Nigeria consistently ranks in the top 10 countries with the highest number of cryptocurrency users.

Regulations

In many countries, regulations are still under construction and are therefore evolving rapidly:

- Tax legislation

- Anti-money laundering/terrorist financing regulations

- Tax and anti-money laundering/terrorist financing regulations

Some countries are changing their legal framework:

- Japan's central bank officially recognizes crypto-currencies as a means of payment (article 2-5 of the amended PSA specifies that virtual currencies are accepted as a means of payment without being legal tender ("a form of payment method, not a legally-recognized currency.").

- In El Salvador, in June 2021, President Nayib Bukele proposed a bill to adopt Bitcoin as legal tender. This was approved by the Legislative Assembly, making El Salvador the first country to legalize a cryptocurrency.

- In the Swiss canton of Zug, bitcoin and ether have been accepted as payment methods for paying taxes since February 2021.

- In the United States, several agencies have issued guidelines concerning crypto-currencies. depending on the agency, they are defined as either securities or currencies by the Securities and Exchange Commission (SEC), commodities by the Commodity Futures Trading Commission (CFTC) and property for tax purposes by the Inland Revenue Service (IRS).Crypto-currencies are also subject to the rules of the Financial Crimes Enforcement Network. In September 2021, according to the US press, the US Treasury was preparing to take sanctions against platforms contributing to illicit cryptocurrency transactions.

- In South Korea, crypto-currency regulations are stringent. Crypto-currency transactions are only allowed from bank accounts with a real name. Until July 2018, crypto-currency transactions are tax-free. However this is in the process of changing.

- In the UK, the government wants to pass a law in 2022 to regulate cryptocurrency advertising and bring it under the control of the Advertising standard authority (ASA). In December 2021, the

ASA already banned advertising for the Fan Token, a cryptocurrency promoted by Arsenal soccer club.

European Union

The European Union has MiCA regulations.

Other regulations apply to crypto-assets in the EU and are of interest to the European Economic Area.

Towards new accounting standards

In the United States

In France, the FASB has been the SEC's authority on accounting standards for CAC40-listed companies since 1973.

On September 6, 2023, the FASB, based on feedback received on its proposed ASU on the accounting and disclosure of certain cryptographic assets. Based on comments received on the proposal, the Board directed its staff to draft a final standard. Under the new guidance, an entity would be required to subsequently measure certain cryptographic assets at fair value, with changes in fair value included in net income during each reporting period.

Large American companies (e.g. Tesla, Microstrategy) have invested heavily in Bitcoin and other cryptocurrencies: Tesla , Microstrategy) have invested massively in Bitcoin or other crypto-currencies, but as these cannot be qualified as currencies, from an accounting point of view they are "*indefinite-lived intangible assets*" *in* accordance with ASC 3502 (i.e., assets must be valued at historical cost less sub-depreciation) unless the entity falls within the scope of the investment company guidelines in ASC 9463 or is a certain type of broker-dealer.

During periods of cryptocurrency impairment, these companies complain that they are unable to record these "declines" as "losses" from an accounting perspective; and cryptocurrency proponents in the Finance sector consider this traditional intangible asset model inadequate because it does not accurately represent the economics of crypto assets, while at the same time complicating impairment accounting because the entities involved must rely on "the lowest observable fair value of a crypto asset during a reporting period. As a result, FASB 5 (in 2023) has proposed amendments that would better reflect the economics of crypto assets held by entities and reduce the complexity and cost of complying with a non-historical cost delaience model under existing ASC 350 requirements."

In 2023, the FASB reaffirmed the majority of the ASU's requirements and guidelines for cryptographic assets based on "a distributed ledger based on blockchain technology", but wants to extend them to cryptographic assets linked to a distributed ledger based on a *technology similar to a blockchain*. It was suggested that these obligations should also be extended "to certain assets that provide rights over other cryptographic assets (e.g., 'wrapped tokens'), the Board ultimately decided not to include these assets within the scope of the final standard".Affected entities will be required, under the final standard, for all fiscal years beginning after December 15, 2024 (including any interim periods within those years, and with earlier adoption permitted) :

- value their cryptographic assets falling within the scope of the guidelines (as amended) at their "fair value, with changes in fair value included in net income for each reporting period".

- Present in their balance sheet the total amount of "cryptographic assets measured at fair value separately from other intangible assets" not measured at fair value.

- Present changes in the fair value of cryptographic assets separately from changes in the book value (e.g., depreciation and amortization) of other intangible assets, including other cryptographic assets not measured at fair value.

- Classify as "cash flow from operating activities" revenues from the almost immediate sale of cryptographic assets that have been "received as non-monetary consideration in the normal course of business (for example, in exchange for the transfer of goods and services to a customer)".

- disclose their significant holdings of cryptographic assets on an annual and interim basis.

The final ASU is expected by the end of 2023, and in the transition phase (when the final standard is adopted) entities will be required to record "a cumulative-effect adjustment to retained earnings (or other appropriate components of equity or net assets) at the beginning of the annual period of adoption. Retrospective restatement would not be required for prior periods".

Centralizing groups

Cryptocurrencies, and blockchain more generally, can lead to various forms of centralizing groupings:

- groupings of "minors

- multi-gigabyte clusters of distributed registers, with thin clients retaining only the latest transactions

- delegation of portfolios and private keys

Transaction fees

Crypto-currency transaction fees depend primarily on the supply of network capacity at the time, versus the currency holder's demand for a faster transaction. The currency holder can choose specific transaction fees, while network entities process transactions in order of highest to lowest fees offered. Crypto-currency exchanges can simplify the process for currency holders by offering prioritized alternatives, and thus determine which fee is likely to result in the transaction being processed within the requested time.

For Ether, transaction fees differ according to computational complexity, bandwidth usage and storage requirements, while Bitcoin transaction fees differ according to transaction size and whether or not the transaction uses SegWit. In September 2018, the median transaction fee for Ether corresponded to $0.017, while for Bitcoin it corresponded to $0.55.

Some crypto-currencies have no transaction fees, relying instead on client-side proof-of-work as a transaction prioritization and anti-spam mechanism.

The two paradoxes of cryptocurrencies

Economist Alexandre Reichart notes two paradoxes associated with cryptocurrencies. The first is that, whether consciously or not, the users and promoters of crypto-currencies are following in the footsteps of Austrian economist Friedrich von Hayek (1899-1992), who was awarded the Nobel Prize for Economic Sciences in 1974. In his book *The Denationalization of Money* (1976), he imagined an economy in which the state would not have a monopoly on issuing money, and in which private currencies would compete with each other. However, it has to be said that *bitcoin*'s users and promoters did not appreciate the explosion of *alt-coins*, which were quickly dubbed "*shitcoins*" by some members of the *bitcoin* community, who promote bitcoin as a currency that competes with legal tender, but do not appreciate competition with bitcoin. Today, however, most members of the *bitcoin* community seem to appreciate, if not tolerate, *alt-coins*.

The second paradox is that, while crypto-currencies were theorized and invented in the 1980s and 1990s by members of the *cypherpunk* and cryptoanarchist communities wishing to create peer-to-peer currencies that would do away with capitalism's own institutions, such as states, central banks and second-tier banks, it has to be said that today crypto-currencies have largely been "reclaimed" by large corporations and central banks. Witness the Diem (formerly Libra) project led by Facebook with other major companies, or the recent interest of monetary authorities in crypto-currencies, with the emergence of central bank digital currencies (CBDCs).

We're a long way from the utopian projects of *cypherpunks* and crypto-anarchists wishing to use technology to bypass capitalist institutions.

Some cryptocurrencies

Community Cryptocurrencies

Exchange platforms

There are centralized (CEX) and decentralized (DEX) cryptocurrency exchange platforms.

Active

- Bittrex (en)
- Binance
- Bitstamp
- BTER
- Coinbase
- Kraken
- Poloniex (en)

Inactive

- Mt. Gox (currently closed, the company having declared bankruptcy in Japan)

- Cryptsy (currently closed following the theft of a large number of bitcoins)

- Vault of Satoshi (closed in 2015)

- Gatecoin (currently closed)

Central bank cryptocurrency

Beyond the new unified cross-border payments system proposed by the IMF, the Bank for International Settlements (BIS) is aiming for a global financial infrastructure to bring together central bank digital currencies (CBDs).

Features, benefits and drawbacks

Benefits

- Designed for the Internet, they offer alternatives to payment systems based on legal tender. They increase the accessibility of online commerce in developing countries.

- Transparency: all transactions are public, with owners and recipients identified by addresses.

- Cryptocurrency cannot easily be counterfeited or spoofed. The encryption protocol is also designed to be highly resistant against most known computer threats, including distributed denial-of-service attacks.

- Transfer fees are sometimes zero, and lower than those charged by payment institutions or money transfer companies (such as Paypal or Western Union).

- Fast transfers from seconds to minutes. Bank transfers take from a few seconds to a few days for large amounts.

- Transfers possible worldwide, regardless of country.

- No intermediary (payment institution, payment services intermediary, bank, custodian): the credited amount is sent directly to the receiving address.

- Any individual or company can transfer cryptocurrency.

- Remote storage of cryptocurrency on a server or download to a medium (e.g. USB key).

- For some cryptocurrencies, the total quantity that can be created is capped, making this type of currency inherently deflationary (the quantity of money can theoretically only decrease over time).

Disadvantages

- Low impact of cryptocurrencies on the general public (~ 150 million USD / day in March 2016 for Bitcoin).

- Payment network underdeveloped but growing.

- Different cryptocurrencies, incompatible with each other, with the development of several types of cryptocurrency in parallel.

- High volatility in a highly unregulated sector, implying vulnerability to scams (example: on March 5, 2021, John McAfee (inventor of the antivirus of the same name) was indicted in the USA (along with an executive advisor on his team) for fraudulently promoting crypto-currencies, and executing *pump-and-dump* market manipulation schemes).

- Risk of deflation/hyperinflation due to insufficient or excessive money creation (e.g. limited quantities of bitcoins).

- Abundance of cryptocurrency scams, jumping 81% in 2021 to $7.7 billion globally, equivalent to the estimated $8 billion in credit card fraud in the US.

- Necessary security (like any deposit or payment account): password, double authentication.

- Cryptocurrency lost (following a download to a USB key or hard disk) is permanently lost.

- Energy consumption due to ever-increasing mining activity.

- Illegal in some countries.

Other features

- Currencies not dependent on banks or central banks.

- Irreversibility of transactions: the receiver of the currency cannot cancel the transaction. Conversely, the principal cannot retract payment.

- No caps or minimums on transfers.

- In the event of death, it is necessary to give the private key to pass on the inheritance.

Banking aspects

The banking lobby opposes the use of this type of currency and defends payment systems using legal tender.

For the Banque de France's Senior Deputy Governor, "crypto-asset infrastructures and activities generate risks comparable to those of traditional financial services, and which are inherent in the provision of financial services, including credit, liquidity and market risks".

In 2022, the Basel Committee called for stricter rules on banks' exposure to digital assets, starting in 2025, to encourage banks to strengthen their balance sheets and avoid another financial crisis. In November 2022, the G20 issued a joint declaration calling for an international framework for regulation along the lines of: same activity as traditional finance, same risk, same regulation.

Power consumption of proof of work

For blockchain technology, every financial exchange must be validated, and in the case of proof-of-work, this involves the calculation of a cryptographic proof, requiring a great deal of decentralized computing power. This computing activity, known as cryptocurrency mining, consumes enormous amounts of electricity. A study by Digiconomist reveals that cryptocurrency required 30.25 TWh of electricity in 2017, a consumption greater than that of many countries. According to Cambridge University, in the 2020s, with an annual consumption of 86.6 terawatt-hours (TWh), the bitcoin network will rank between Belgium (81.2 TWh/year) and the Philippines (90.9 TWh/year).

In 2020, three quarters of the world's mining capacity is based in China (before the legal changes concerning cryptocurrencies); 27% of Chinese miners are in Sichuan, a province with high low-carbon hydroelectric production, but 43% are in Xinjiang, where 80% of electricity comes from coal-fired power plants. China's major renewable energy source, hydroelectricity, is only available at low cost in the wet season. For the rest of the year, electricity is mainly generated by coal.

A study carried out by Chinese scientists and published in April 2021 in the scientific journal Nature Communications reveals that in 2020, mining was 78.9% carried out in China; CO_2 emissions due to mining over the period from January 1, 2016 to June 30, 2018 are estimated at 13 million tonnes, equivalent to Denmark's annual emissions; according to the simulations in this study, mining energy consumption in China could reach 297 TWh in 2024, or 5.4% of China's electricity production, causing CO_2 emissions of 130 million tonnes, equivalent to those of the Czech Republic and Qatar.

Since June 2021, China has been on a crusade against bitcoin production, with authorities in the Sichuan region demanding the immediate closure of 26 mining farms. Sichuan is the second largest bitcoin mining province, according to data compiled by Cambridge University. Before Sichuan, which draws its electricity from hydroelectric dams, other provinces such as Xinjiang, Inner Mongolia, Qinghai and Yunnan ordered measures against bitcoin mining. According to the Communist Party daily "Global Times", 90% of Chinese facilities have been shut down in recent weeks.

Faced with an energy crisis, Kosovo decided in January 2022 to ban cryptocurrency mining on its soil.

Validating transactions on the *blockchain* is energy-intensive, and no alternative protocol to *proof-of-work* (PoW) has been found that would enable a decentralized, public, secure cryptocurrency with a negligible carbon footprint.

Other books by United Library

https://campsite.bio/unitedlibrary

9 789464 902945